Published by Compass, an imprint of Brigantine Media
211 North Avenue, Saint Johnsbury, Vermont 05819

Cover and book design by Jacob L. Grant

If you would like to use the book with multiple teachers, please have your school purchase a site
license for the downloadable version.

For more information about site licenses, contact:

Brigantine Media
211 North Avenue
Saint Johnsbury, Vermont 05819
Phone: 802-751-8802
E-mail: neil@brigantinemedia.com
Website: www.brigantinemedia.com

INTRODUCTION

There are four kinds of sentences:

I **simple**

II **compound**

III **complex**

IV **compound-complex**

This document includes **explanations** of each kind of sentence with **examples** to make the point, and **exercises** for the students.

EXPLANATIONS

The explanations are designed to show **how sentence structure works** and **why it matters**. You can use the explanations in class to help teach your students, or print them as a handout.

EXAMPLES

The examples demonstrate the specific grammar points to cover in class.

EXERCISES

The exercises for your students will help ensure that your students have learned to identify different kinds of sentences and to think creatively about the way sentences work.

There are two kinds of exercises:

DEVELOPING SKILLS

These exercises make sure students understand the basic principles involved. Print these exercises for students to work with, either in class or as homework. Answers and discussion material for the teacher follow on a separate sheet.

DEVELOPING MASTERY

These exercises are to practice how style affects content. Each of these exercises limits the constructions the students may use, thus making them force their meaning through a syntactical demand.

Introduce the Developing Mastery exercises only after you are comfortable that your students have mastered the Developing Skills exercises. The Developing Mastery exercises incorporate knowledge of all four kinds of sentences.

The example I use when explaining the purpose of Developing Mastery exercises is a sonnet: a fourteen-line poem in iambic pentameter in which every other line rhymes, except the rhyming couplet at the end. If the poet follows the rules, the structure of the sonnet pushes her into ideas that she didn't anticipate, and (on a good day) into a rhyming couplet better than anything she anticipated when plunging into the poem. **The moral**: structure can support and enhance meaning if you engage in a partnership with its demands.

Developing Mastery exercises III, IV, and V require considerable stylistic control (page 40). These exercises can be assigned as homework, or they can be done by oral cooperation in class.

Students who are really struggling with the Developing Mastery exercises should be given easier versions (for example, the 300-word essays can be reduced to 100 words or even 50, with bonus points added for getting it and going on), but they should be encouraged to try them. Since students may write about anything they wish, no answers can be provided here. My guideline is that nonsense is encouraged, but "keep it clean" is the order of the day.

● STRATEGIC CLASSROOM SUGGESTIONS

If possible, project a **blank computer page** on a screen everybody can see, and furnish the class with a **wireless keyboard** that gets passed around so everybody can type. Arrange the students in a circle or u-shape (not rows), and put yourself at the opposite side of the circle from the screen. Project sentences, right and wrong, onto the screen for discussion. Allow (but don't force!) students to type their answers onto the screen, assuring them that nobody will jeer if they're wrong. Arranging the classroom in this fashion makes you a fellow pilgrim on the road to truth, rather than an authority figure who stands at the board and dictates. By making learning sentence structure into an interactive endeavor, you can **break down the passivity and resentment** with which students often greet grammar lessons. Encourage participation by getting the students to write a ridiculously long simple sentence by oral cooperation, or by getting each one of them to write one sentence apiece in Exercise III on page 40, writing an essay all in simple sentences. They will see the limitations of different sentence structures very quickly if they are allowed to play with them.

● WHY SENTENCE STRUCTURE MATTERS

In general, basic sentence structure matters because it is the only tool you have to make written meaning clear. With writing, as with any other skilled work, mastery of tools is essential to creating a good finished product. You can muddle along with the wrong tools—pliers instead of a wrench, safety pins instead of buttons—but the result may very well evoke scorn or laughter. Similarly, readers can probably understand what you say if you say it badly, but consistent misuse of sentence structure undermines readers' trust of your intelligence and analytical ability.

To write sentences that evoke respect (and in the long term, trust) in your reader, you need to understand what a given structure is designed to support. You also need to understand what the power points of a sentence are and how to put the sentence's most important words in the syntactically powerful places.

I. THE SIMPLE SENTENCE

● EXPLANATION

HOW IT WORKS

A **simple sentence is composed of a single clause**. By definition, a clause contains a subject and a predicate.

At its most simple, a simple sentence consists of a simple subject and a simple predicate:

> Hippogriffs eat.
>
> Peasants scream.

The simple subject of a sentence is the agent or topic of the sentence's action. The simple predicate is the verb.

Both the simple subject and the simple predicate can be expanded with modifiers, objects, or complements. The expanded forms are called complete subjects and complete predicates.

Here are some examples of complete subjects with simple predicates.

> Hippogriffs, fantastic combinations of horses and griffins, eat.
>
> Cruising through little towns and causing great havoc, hippogriffs eat.
>
> Cruising through little towns and causing great havoc, hippogriffs, fantastic combinations of horses and griffins, eat.

Here are some examples of simple subjects with complete predicates.

Hippogriffs eat peasants.

Peasants scream with anguish.

Peasants scream with anguish, hide under bushes, and crawl into holes to escape destruction.

As the examples above prove, **a simple sentence is not necessarily short**. Nor is its topic necessarily simple. And as Exercise III on page 40 will prove, it is not necessarily simple to write. When constructing simple sentences, you may use only one subject and predicate.

You may put as many agents into your subject as you wish, *so long as they all govern a single verb*:

Hippogriffs, dragons, and vampires are fantastic creatures.

You may use as many verbs as you wish *so long as they are all performed by the subject*.

The hippogriff flew, dove, lost his balance, and crashed into a cliff.

You may add as many modifiers and modifying phrases as you wish *so long as none of them contains its own subject and predicate*.

The gross, grizzly hippogriff with an extra pair of wings crashed into the rock hanging over the edge of the cliff.

You may NOT add modifying clauses with their own subjects and predicates.

The hippogriff ~~that had extra wings~~ crashed into a cliff.

The hippogriff ate peasants ~~when it got hungry~~.

WHY IT MATTERS

A simple sentence is the correct tool for:

Expressing short statements of truth that stick in the mind. These are variously called epigrams, proverbs, maxims, aphorisms—or in common parlance, one-liners.

Remarriage is a triumph of hope over experience.

Patriotism is the last refuge of scoundrels.

The only way to get rid of temptation is to yield to it.

ǁ **Presenting simple factual statements** without embellishment.

> Napoleon lost the Battle of Waterloo.
>
> Emperor Frederick Barbarossa drowned in a small stream.
>
> Henry VIII married six wives, divorced one, lost one in childbirth, set one aside, executed two, and predeceased the last.

ǁǁ **Controlling the pace** of a sentence's action.

If a single subject performs a number of verbs in a row, the pace of the sentence mimics the fast pace of the action:

> The maiden rushed up the stairs, ran down the hall, broke open the last door, tore the Ineffective Knight from the jaws of the jabberwock, dashed down to his waiting horse with him swooning over her shoulder, and rode to safety.

A series of short sentences slows the pace, thus supporting a situation that describes a hiatus in the action:

> He saw the hippogriff. His hand moved to his sword. He thought of the SPCA. He hesitated. That was a mistake.

What a simple sentence can't do, because it is limited to a single subject and predicate, is:

ǀ Make comparisons

ǁ Describe causal relations

ǁǁ Subordinate one idea to another

These situations are handled by compound and complex sentences.

SIMPLE SENTENCE EXERCISES

Circle the simple subject and the verb in each of the sentences below.
Then put brackets around the complete predicate of each sentence.

(If you identify the simple subject, the predicate, and the verb, the complete subject will appear naturally.)

I   Ever a poor politician, Charles I lost his head.

II   Screaming loudly and brandishing a pistol, Emily ran out the door in a lace whatchamacallit.

III   The Ancient Mariner wore an albatross around his neck for weeks on end.

IV   Having lived in England for thirty-seven years, four months, two weeks, one hour and thirty-two seconds, Henry left that hallowed country regretfully.

V   According to Joe, Henry's nephew's half-brother's second cousin Albert was actually Aunt Rhoda's step-nephew by marriage.

VI   Under the influence of drugs, Samuel Taylor Coleridge wrote "Kubla Khan."

VII   Galileo, the great astronomer confined to house arrest for insulting the pope, lost his sight in the last years of his life.

Underline all the nouns in the predicates of the sentences below.

I   Galloping around the field, the centaur called the horse following him a plug.

II   Having eaten five vampire bats for breakfast, the wolf asked for two antacids and a glass of milk.

III   A mass noun like *sawdust* has no plural.

IV   Working for McDonald's for the first time in her life, the girl accidentally made all kinds of dreadful mistakes, tallying up the accounts all wrong.

V   Werewolves, turning from men into wolves and back again at the drop of a hat, first appear in the story of Lycaon in Ovid's *Metamorphoses*, an epic poem about changes in form written in Rome shortly after the birth of Christ.

VI   An oxymoron is a contradiction in terms, not a stupid bovine creature.

VII   The pope crowned Charlemagne King of the Franks in the year 800.

VIII   The Queen gave Albert's uncle thirty florins in return for his distinguished service.

IX   The bandit chieftain appointed Joe cock of the walk and prince of thieves.

**Circle the simple subject and the verb in each of the sentences below.
Then put brackets around the complete predicate of each sentence.**

(If you identify the simple subject, the predicate, and the verb, the complete subject will appear naturally.)

The point here is to make sure students get the idea of the parts of a simple sentence. Note that the predicate is the verb and everything that follows it. What has not been put in brackets is the complete subject.

I   Ever a poor politician, (Charles I) [(lost) his head].

II   Screaming loudly and brandishing a pistol, (Emily) [(ran) out the door in a lace whatchamacallit.]

III   (The Ancient Mariner) [(wore) an albatross around his neck for weeks on end.]

IV   Having lived in England for thirty-seven years, four months, two weeks, one hour and thirty-two seconds, (Henry) [(left) that hallowed country regretfully.]

V   According to Joe, Henry's nephew's half-brother's second cousin (Albert) [(was) actually Aunt Rhoda's step-nephew by marriage.]

VI   Under the influence of drugs, (Samuel Taylor Coleridge) [(wrote) "Kubla Khan."]

VII   (Galileo,) the great astronomer confined to house arrest for insulting the pope, [(lost) his sight in the last years of his life.]

Underline all the nouns in the predicates of the sentences below.

Have students circle the verb first, so they know where the predicate starts. Make it clear that nouns in the complete subject don't count. In 20 years, NO student has ever spotted all the nouns. Nouns disappear in predicates, mainly because they appear in phrases. The moral: do not put important nouns in a predicate phrase—readers read right over them.

I   Galloping around the field, the centaur called the <u>horse</u> following him a <u>plug</u>.

II   Having eaten five vampire bats for breakfast, the wolf asked for two <u>antacids</u> and a <u>glass</u> of <u>milk</u>.

III   A mass noun like *sawdust* has no <u>plural</u>.

IV   Working for McDonald's for the first time in her life, the girl accidentally made all <u>kinds</u> of dreadful <u>mistakes</u>, tallying up the <u>accounts</u> all wrong.

V Werewolves, turning from men into wolves and back again at the drop of a hat, first appear in the story of Lycaon in Ovid's *Metamorphoses*, an epic poem about changes in form written in Rome shortly after the birth of Christ.

VI An oxymoron is a contradiction in terms, not a stupid bovine creature.

VII The pope crowned Charlemagne king of the Franks in the year 800.

VIII The queen gave Albert's uncle thirty florins in return for his distinguished service.

IX The bandit chieftain appointed Joe cock of the walk and prince of thieves.

II. THE COMPOUND SENTENCE

● EXPLANATION

HOW IT WORKS

A **compound sentence is composed of two (or more) independent clauses** that are syntactically linked either by a comma and a coordinating conjunction (and, but, for, so) or by a semicolon.

A clause, by definition, has a subject and a predicate. An **independent clause** is a clause that can be taken out of a longer sentence and remain a sentence in its own right without changing any of its words. Essentially, an independent clause is a simple sentence that has changed its name because making it part of another kind of sentence has changed its syntactical function.

Simple sentences:

> The hippogriffs chased the beautiful maiden.
>
> The knight fought them ineffectively.

Compound sentences:

Independent clause	Coordinating Conjunction	Independent clause
The hippogriffs chased the beautiful maiden,	*and*	the knight fought them ineffectively.
The hippogriffs chased the beautiful maiden,	*but*	the knight fought them ineffectively.

The hippogriffs chased the beautiful maiden,	*for*	the knight fought them ineffectively.
The hippogriffs chased the beautiful maiden,	*so*	the knight fought them ineffectively.
The hippogriffs chased the beautiful maiden	*;*	the knight fought them ineffectively.

As with simple sentences, you may add any modifying words or phrases to either of the independent clauses, and the sentence will remain compound. (The outcome, though syntactically correct, will not be stylistically impressive.)

> The astoundingly huge hippogriffs, claws extended, teeth gnashing, chased the beautiful maiden over the hill, through the river and into the forest, and the overwrought young knight, his red hair gleaming in the dying light, fought them every step of the way with more bravado than skill.

The **coordinating conjunction** that links the two independent clauses has more effect on the meaning of the sentence than you might think.

And simply links the clauses—its use in the sentence above implies a dispassionate observer.

But implies reversal—it implies that the knight's appearance changed the situation.

For implies causality—it implies that the hippogriffs attacked the maiden because the knight showed up. Generally, using "for" instead of "because" is not a good idea.

So implies consequence—the attack gave the knight something to do.

A **semicolon** links the two independent clauses without comment; its presence, however, suggests that the link is more than syntactical. A semicolon often implies causality.

Separating two independent clauses with a comma instead of a comma and a coordinating conjunction or a semicolon is a very common error—that great syntactical monster, the **Comma Splice.**

> The hippogriffs chased the beautiful maiden, the knight fought them ineffectively.

WHY IT MATTERS

A compound sentence implies that its independent clauses contain material of equal importance. Used correctly, it tells your reader to pay attention to both its halves.

✓ Galileo popularized the Copernican view of the solar system, but the common view of the universe changed slowly in the seventeenth century.

The sentence structure implies that you have two equally important things to say: 1) Galileo popularized the idea of a heliocentric universe, and 2) it took a long time for laymen to believe him. "But" tells the reader to expect a reversal. All is well.

Suppose, however, you put two ideas of unequal importance into a compound sentence:

✗ Milton began *Paradise Lost*, and he was Latin Secretary to Oliver Cromwell.

The sentence structure simply links two facts without relating them to each other; it thus implies that both facts are equally important, but you don't know why. All is not well.

What is needed here is a complex sentence, not a compound sentence:

✓ Milton began *Paradise Lost* when he was Latin Secretary to Oliver Cromwell.

Now the second idea modifies the first; the sentence structure supports the information and implies authorial knowledge.

A **compound sentence** is not designed to express causality. Nor is it designed to subordinate one idea to another. It can, however, **express sequential action, reversal, or results** with the employment of a conjunctive adverb, which connects two independent clauses while maintaining the equality the sentence choice implies. Here is a list of conjunctive adverbs:

accordingly	however	now
also	instead	otherwise
anyway	likewise	still
besides	meanwhile	similarly
consequently	moreover	subsequently
finally	namely	then
further	nevertheless	thereafter
furthermore	next	therefore
hence	nonetheless	thus

Conjunctive adverbs are familiar to teachers mainly through their misuse. Students often confuse them with subordinating conjunctions (page 17) and thus innocently use them after commas. The result, once again, is the monster Comma Splice.

, The knight's sword broke, therefore/accordingly/thereafter/consequently the hippogriff ate him.

The maiden crawled into a small cave, otherwise the hippogriff would have eaten her, too.

The knight's sword broke; consequently, the hippogriff ate him.

The maiden crawled into a small cave; otherwise the hippogriff would have eaten her, too.

"Also," though technically correct, denotes afterthought rather than deeper thought. Students should be encouraged to use "furthermore" or "moreover" instead.

The maiden found a sword in the cave; also, she knew how to use it.

The maiden found a sword in the cave; moreover/furthermore, she knew how to use it.

Stylistically, the **compound sentence**, accompanied by parallel structure, can be built very nicely into **a periodic sentence**—a device found most often in political speeches:

We will feed the hungry; we will employ the masses; we will lead the world; and we will become a great nation!

But it's perfectly all right (if a bit rhetorical) in honest hands.

Knowledge gives us wisdom; wisdom gives us compassion; compassion gives us humanity.

A compound sentence is often confused with a simple sentence with a compound verb. A compound sentence has *two* subjects doing *two different things,* and the coordinating conjunction between the two independent clauses is preceded by a comma. If a *single* subject does *two* things, it's a simple sentence, and the "and" in the compound verb is NOT preceded by a comma.

The hippogriff roared loudly, and the maiden ran fast.
(compound sentence; comma)

The hippogriff roared and chased the fleeing maiden.
(compound verb; no comma)

A modifying phrase that precedes the subject of a sentence should be separated from it by a comma.

Having seen the maiden in the fields, the hippogriff attacked her hungrily.

COMPOUND SENTENCE EXERCISES

Punctuate the following sentences.

I   Joe is a handsome boy with cheeks of tan and Sarah is a charming little girl with a curl in the middle of her forehead.

II   Macroeconomics is the study of major countries' economies and microeconomics is the study of businesses, families, and budgets.

III   The dragon circled a couple of times and dove at the maiden but the maiden was gathering flowers and didn't notice.

IV   The dragon consumed the maiden with lightning speed and the knight in shining armor arrived too late to save her.

V   The knight killed the dragon and cleaned up the mess and he shed bitter tears for his lost love.

VI   The knight rode toward the castle and the dragon's mate attacked him.

VII   Seizing his sword in his trusty right hand he finished her off with one blow.

VIII   He wiped the sweat from his brow and rode on in search of the dragons' lair.

IX   Having found the lair and its contents of eleven dragons' eggs the knight committed small-time genocide.

X   At the end of a long day of slaughtering dragons and mourning his love the knight spent a couple of hours in the local pub.

Punctuate the following sentences.

I   Joe is a handsome boy with cheeks of tan, and Sarah is a charming little girl with a curl in the middle of her forehead.

II   Macroeconomics is the study of major countries' economies, and microeconomics is the study of businesses, families, and budgets.

III   The dragon circled a couple of times and dove at the maiden, but the maiden was gathering flowers and didn't notice.
Only one comma; maiden and dragon each did two things.

IV   The dragon consumed the maiden with lightning speed, and the knight in shining armor arrived too late to save her.

V   The knight killed the dragon and cleaned up the mess, and he shed bitter tears for his lost love.
If they say this sounds terrible, they're right. Too many "ands"—a common fault in student writing.

VI   The knight rode toward the castle, and the dragon's mate attacked him.

VII   Seizing his sword in his trusty right hand, he finished her off with one blow.

VIII   He wiped the sweat from his brow and rode on in search of the dragons' lair.
No comma; he did two things.

IX   Having found the lair and its contents of eleven dragons' eggs, the knight committed small-time genocide.

X   At the end of a long day of slaughtering dragons and mourning his love, the knight spent a couple of hours in the local pub.

III. THE COMPLEX SENTENCE

● EXPLANATION

HOW IT WORKS

A **complex sentence is composed of an independent clause and one or more dependent clauses**.

An independent clause (with the requisite subject and predicate) can be taken out of a longer sentence and remain a sentence in its own right without changing any of its words. Essentially, an independent clause is a simple sentence that has changed its name because it has changed its syntactical function.

A dependent clause contains its own subject and predicate, but it also contains a key word that makes its syntactical place in the sentence depend on the independent clause. It therefore *cannot* remain a sentence in its own right if it is taken out of a complex sentence without changing any of its words. A **dependent clause that appears on its own is called a sentence fragment.**

Here are a variety of sentence fragments. They can be attached to independent clauses to make complex sentences in different ways.

Fragment	Complex sentence
Because hippogriffs cruise at night.	**Because** hippogriffs cruise at night, you should jog in the morning.
Unless owls court pussycats.	**Unless** owls court pussycats, pea green boats will languish.
That has wings.	A hippogriff is a horse-griffin cross that has wings.

Which made the knight hungry.	The maiden put the kettle on, which made the knight hungry.
Whether pigs can fly.	I don't know whether pigs can fly.
What I mean.	I rarely say what I mean.

As the pairs of examples above illustrate, there are three kinds of dependent clauses: adverb/subordinate clauses, adjective/relative clauses, and noun clauses. Of these, the noun clause is the most difficult to explain; teachers often discuss only adverb (subordinate) and adjective (relative) clauses. Such omission will leave you unable to explain the syntax of familiar sentences like "That's not what I meant," or "I wonder why he is so late," so the noun clause is included here.

● THE ADVERB/SUBORDINATE CLAUSE

An adverb/subordinate clause consists of a subject, a predicate, and (crucially) a subordinating conjunction that attaches it to an independent clause. Its double name describes both its functions: it is subordinate to the independent clause; and it works as a corporation adverb, indicating where, when, why, and how the action in the independent clause took place.

> Although this is a subordinate clause, this clause is independent.

> Readers pay attention to this clause because this one is subordinate.

Subordinating conjunctions comprise a closed class of words whose function is to join clauses by making one clause dependent on another. Below is a list of them.

after	if only	that
although	in order that	though
as	insofar as	till
as long as	in that	unless
as soon as	lest	until
as if	no matter how	when
as though	now that	whenever
because	once	whereas
before	provided that	wherever
even if	since	while
even though	so that	why
if	than	

Warning: Some words that act as subordinating conjunctions also serve other functions in different syntactical situations; they thus have different names. For example:

After the greyhound devoured the metal rabbit, it got sick. (subordinating conjunction)

After that incident, the greyhound stopped running. (preposition)

Jennifer was once a white rabbit. (adverb)

Once Jennifer became human, she disliked rabbit stew. (subordinating conjunction)

Jennifer dove into a hole, and I haven't seen her since. (adverb)

Since Jennifer dove into a hole, the earth has moved oddly. (subordinating conjunction)

WHY IT MATTERS

Because it is flexible, the complex sentence is the one people write most frequently, and so if it is misused, the reader will distrust the author's understanding of the content. Your students don't want to evoke such distrust, especially in letters of application or reports for the boss, so they should be cautioned to avoid the following frequently found problems:

I. Fragments

The problem is one of recognition. A sentence that begins with a subordinating conjunction *must* be complex; it will have to have an independent clause. If all else fails, start the sentence with the subject; a sentence that starts with the subject cannot be a fragment.

A fragment will not always be short. Sometimes in the heat of composition, a writer piles information into a sentence, suddenly realizes it has been going on for a long time, and (fatally) sticks in a period.

While the defeat of the most valorous knight in the kingdom appeared to be a disaster, one more discouraging to the maidens watching and wishing to give advice but not daring to than anything previously experienced in their cloistered lives.

Stop. Think. What is the subject of the sentence? Put it up front. The defeat of the most valorous knight in the kingdom… Is that the subject? Or maybe you want the valorous knight's defeat to be the subject. Or maybe the disaster or the maidens should be the subject. The subject that is chosen by the writer will greatly affect the rest of the sentence, which has gone wrong partly because the writer wasn't quite sure what the subject should be. A little trial and error with sentence subjects will generally straighten this out; at that point, it will be comparatively easy to fix the sentence.

II. Punctuation difficulties

The rules here, though often confused, are straightforward.

If the adverb/subordinate clause <u>precedes</u> the independent clause, it <u>must</u> be separated from it by a comma.

> When he fell in love with Cinderella, the prince was euphoric.

> If Cinderella's fairy godmother hadn't given her a carriage, she couldn't have made it to the ball.

If the adverb/subordinate clause <u>follows</u> the independent clause, the comma depends on the relationship of the two clauses:

If the subordinate clause **specifies the circumstances of the situation** (thereby restricting it), there is **no comma** between clauses.

> The prince was euphoric when he fell in love with Cinderella.

> Cinderella couldn't have made it to the ball if her fairy godmother had given her a carriage.

If the subordinate/adverb clause **merely adds information or a comment,** it **is** separated from the independent clause by a comma.

> Cinderella was self-conscious about her garlicky hands, if you ask me.

> Cinderella danced her best, since she really needed to escape her dysfunctional family.

If you are not sure whether the subordinate clause restricts the independent clause, put it first; the comma will then be automatic.

III. Misuse and non-use of as

a. *I don't see as it was wrong.* Here, *as* has been made to replace *that.* This common gentrification is incorrect: *as* starts an adverbial clause; *that* starts a noun clause, which is what's needed in this sentence. The particulars are complicated, but the rule is straightforward: phrases like *I can't say, I don't see* should be followed by *that,* not *as.*

> *I don't see that it was wrong.*

> *I can't say that it made much difference.*

b. *As the knight yelled, the maiden ran to help.* There is nothing wrong grammatically, here, but *as* can mean either *while* or *because*—and in this case it's not clear which it means. Clarify the meaning by using the subordinating conjunction that best expresses it.

While the knight yelled, the maiden ran to help.

Because the knight yelled, the maiden ran to help.

c. *He got in trouble, just like I said.* ✗ Here, *like*, which is a preposition, is used in place of *as*, which in this context is a subordinating conjunction. Mistakes of this kind are legion, because *like* has a wonderful colloquial flair that is used all the time in spoken English.

He grooms his horse like I brush my hair.

She cleans the house like dirt was a sin.

They act like they invented marriage.

It looks like it's going to rain.

There is no need to purge spoken English of these colloquialisms. In essays, letters of application, business reports, and SAT exams, however, follow these rules:

- Do not start a subordinate clause with *like*.

- Do not assume you can just replace *like* with *as* or *as if*.

  They act as if they invented marriage. ✓ But

  He grooms his dog as if [as] I brush my hair. ✗

When in doubt, recast the sentence.

- Do not start clauses with *unlike*.

  Unlike the weatherman promised, it rained. ✗

  Unlike everybody expected, the Ineffective Knight was a great general. ✗

Instead, recast the sentence.

  The weatherman promised sun, but it rained. ✓

  Nobody expected the Ineffective Knight to be a great general. ✓

It is, of course, perfectly permissible to start *phrases* with *like* or *unlike*.

  Like his father, the Ineffective Knight was a great general. ✓

  Unlike his father, the Ineffective Knight was a slob. ✓

IV. Keep subordinate ideas in the subordinate clause

Readers habitually skip over a subordinate clause and look for meaning in the independent clause. It follows that to put important points in a subordinate clause is to mislead your reader and possibly yourself. Beware. This is remarkably easy to do.

> *When the captured king escaped political execution, the Ineffective Knight spoke for him.*
>
> *The captured king escaped political execution when the Ineffective Knight spoke for him.*

● THE ADJECTIVE/ RELATIVE CLAUSE

An adjective/relative clause, like all clauses, has its own subject and predicate, but it **cannot stand on its own without a change in words.** It is joined (related) to the independent clause by a relative pronoun. It is called an adjective clause because it serves as a corporation adjective that modifies either the noun that precedes it or the whole independent clause.

> A simple sentence that is interrupted by a relative clause automatically becomes complex.
>
> A relative clause often modifies the whole independent clause, which sometimes confuses grammar students.
>
> A student who encounters relative clauses often encounters inflection problems.
>
> A student to whom relative clauses are confusing often despairs.
>
> A person whose syntactical skills are weak often inflects "who" incorrectly.

There are five relative pronouns:

> *that, which*—refer to objects, ideas, and things
> *who, whom, whose*—refer to people

The pronouns that refer to people inflect; that is, their endings vary according to their syntactical function in the clause. *Who* is a subject; *whom* is an object; *whose* is possessive.

WHY IT MATTERS

The adjective/relative clause is so useful that you tend to write it without even being aware of it—until you run into problems with restriction or case. These problems are so ubiquitous that you cannot always trust your ear (*who* or *whom*? *that* or *which*?). Again, misuse of a construction evokes distrust in the reader, so to be convincing, your students need to master the principles below:

I. Restriction

that or *which*? Commas or no commas?

Some relative clauses and phrases limit the identity or meaning of words they modify. These are called **restrictive clauses or phrases**; if they are removed from the sentence, its meaning changes—or, in some cases, all but disappears.

A man who has two heads has trouble finding a job.

A man has trouble finding a job.

A restrictive clause is <u>not</u> set off from the independent clause by commas. Putting commas around a restrictive clause implies that its presence in the sentence is inessential to its meaning. In the case above, it isn't.

Restrictive clauses that refer to objects should start with *that*, not *which*. It follows that you should not set *that* clauses off with commas.

A relative clause that restricts the meaning of the subject

should not be set off by commas.

A clause or phrase that has no effect on the sentence's meaning, simply adding information that might be interesting, is **non-restrictive**. Because it can be removed from the sentence, a non-restrictive clause <u>must</u> be set off from the sentence by commas.

Non-restrictive clauses that deal with things should start with *which*, not *that*. It follows that you should use commas to set off clauses starting with *which*.

A non-restrictive relative clause, which can be left out without changing the meaning of the sentence, should be set off by commas.

In some cases, the punctuation of otherwise identical relative clauses changes the meaning of the sentence.

All old people who have poor eyesight should not drive.
(Restrictive—only old people with poor vision should not drive.)

All old people, who have poor eyesight, should not drive.
(Non-restrictive—implies that all old people have poor vision and that no old people should drive. AARP will have your hide.)

The moral: if your subject refers to a group, a restrictive clause will allow you to discuss *a sub-group* within it; a non-restrictive clause requires you to discuss *all of it*.

In general, if the subject of the independent clause has already been identified in some way (a proper noun, a reference in the preceding sentence), the relative clause that follows it will be non-restrictive.

King Garamond, who expects far too much of his son, is bound to be disappointed.

The guy with the crown, who expects far too much of his son, is bound to be disappointed.

An unidentified subject, however, needs to be identified by a restrictive relative clause.

A king who expects far too much of his son is bound to be disappointed.

II. Inflection

who or *whom?*

Inflection, in grammar, **is a variation in a word's form**. In English, the most familiar inflection occurs in verbs (*I go; I went; I have gone*), and in number—the singular and plural—of nouns (one *child*; two *children* / one *rose*; two *roses*). Nouns and pronouns have a special inflection of **case**, which means their form varies according to their syntactical use.

Nouns inflect this way only in the possessive (*lady, lady's, ladies'*); but pronouns have subjective, objective and possessive forms of their own (who; whom; whose). In relative clauses, it is necessary to use the right case in referring to the noun modified.

Who does double duty as a relative pronoun and the subject of its own clause.

I tossed the man who stole my iPod to the hippogriffs.

Whose refers to something possessed by the subject. It modifies the subject of its own clause.

The knight whose shoes didn't match fell over his feet at an inopportune moment.

Whom is an object, either of a verb or of a preposition; it is thus part of the predicate of its own clause, not the subject.

The knight whom the lady adored was a great disappointment to her father.

The Ineffective Knight, upon whom disasters routinely fell, liked ladies better than fathers.

(Think: she adored him; disasters fell upon him. *Him,* therefore *whom*.)

A note of warning:
Do not let the rules governing *whom* lead you to use *whomever* instead of *whoever*. *Whoever* begins

noun clauses. Thus, while *whomever* may seem appropriate as the object of a preposition, actually the whole clause is the object, and *whoever* is its subject.

> The king offered golden spurs to whoever conquered the hippogriff.

> The maiden promised to love whoever conquered the hippogriff.

● THE NOUN CLAUSE

A **noun clause** is a corporation noun; like all clauses, it has its own subject and predicate, and like adjective clauses, it is related to the independent clause by a relative pronoun. It is different from adverb and adjective clauses because instead of acting like a modifier, it **substitutes for a single-word noun in any syntactical place a noun can be used.**

> **Subject**: Whoever gets to the bat station first should call the belfry.

> **Direct Object**: I wonder why people don't use pigeons instead of bats.

> **Indirect Object**: I gave whatever her name was an engagement ring.

> **Object of Preposition**: I disagree with what most people say about hippogriffs.

Note that each one of the noun clauses could be replaced by a single noun, though the meaning would change considerably:

> *Joe* should call the belfry.

> I wonder about *the use of pigeons instead of bats.*

> I gave *my love* an engagement ring.

> I disagree with *common hippogriff beliefs.*

Noun clauses are introduced by relative pronouns, almost all of which also serve other syntactical functions: that, what, whatever, whoever, why (**not** *whenever* or *wherever*, which start subordinate/adverb clauses).

Noun clauses occur most usually and gracefully in indirect discourse or statements of wish, wonder, belief, or speculation.

> Joe said that his horse had five legs.

> The judge couldn't believe that his horse could do such lovely dressage.

I wish my horse had five legs.
(Note that the word "that" has been left out. It's still a noun clause.)

The noun clause is used least gracefully as a sentence subject. Rephrase!

    ✗ What the problem is is that we need more information.

    ✓ If we want to solve the problem, we need more information.

It is also graceless as the object of a preposition.

    ✗ We talked about whether we should take a trip or not.

    ✓ We discussed taking a trip.

The noun clause can also be used in **an expletive**, which is a dummy construction that takes the place of the "true" subject of a sentence by beginning the sentence with *it is* or *there are*.

It is true that the Ineffective Knight was an odd fellow.

There is a myth that hippogriffs don't exist.

In cases like these, the subject of the sentence is not *it* but the noun clause that follows the expletive.

That the Ineffective Knight was an odd fellow is true.

That hippogriffs don't exist is a myth.

In some cases expletives are permissible—even desirable—because they enable the writer to emphasize a general sentiment. For example, Jane Austen's *Pride and Prejudice* begins with a splendidly ironic expletive: "It is a truth universally acknowledged, that a single man in possession of a good fortune must be in want of a wife."

That said, however, expletives are wordy and often awkward—and worst of all, addictive. Students groping for a true subject will often begin sentences with such hopeful expletives as *It is true that, It is clear that, There is no question that,* and worst of all, *The fact that.* Encourage them to delete expletives in revision (not in the initial heat of composition, when anything that comes from the brain should go onto the screen). The sentences above could easily read:

The Ineffective Knight was an odd fellow.

Hippogriffs certainly do exist.

WHY IT MATTERS

Noun clauses, though they are easily and gracefully used in the predicates of sentences, frequently appear as subjects. Somehow, beginning a sentence with clauses like *What the goal of the resolution is*, or *That the Democratic party appeared to be degenerating*, or *Whether the current situation merits discussion* sounds professional and sophisticated.

> ✗ What the goal of the resolution is is unclear from the committee's notes.

> ✗ That the Democratic party appears to be degenerating is the outcome of inconsistent ideology.

> ✗ Whether the current situation merits discussion is open to investigation.

Do not let your students be deceived. Noun clauses in the subject slot of a sentence permit a kind of verbal smoke screen that enables writers to appear learned without saying anything. That's a situation that fools not only the reader but the writer. Encourage your students to be honest with themselves and with others. Show them how to use nouns as subjects. Show them what happens when people don't say who did what to whom.

> ✓ The committee's notes don't record the resolution accurately.

> ✓ Inconsistent ideology is weakening the Democratic party.

> ✓ Maybe we should take a good look at the situation.

COMPLEX SENTENCE EXERCISES

ADVERB/SUBORDINATE CLAUSE EXERCISES:

Correct the following sentences.

I   Unlike my mother told me, babies don't come from storks.

II   I wish I had a golden carriage like Cinderella did.

III   If the knight had married the maiden, like he said he would, she wouldn't be a single parent.

IV   That maiden combs her hair like the queen pulled a dagger on her.

V   Unlike the war with the hippogriffs, the Ineffective Knight soundly defeated the invading army.

VI   I can't see as the passage of time has made maidens any smarter.

Combine the simple sentences below first into compound sentences, then into complex sentences with subordinate/adverb clauses. You may switch the order of the clauses any way you want, and you may use pronouns instead of repeating names.

I   The Ineffective Knight was an odd fellow. His use of hippogriffs as airborne cavalry saved the kingdom from certain defeat.

II   The great recorder of the Ineffective Knight's deeds spent several years in jail for lying under oath. He wrote his epic poem to reflect on the difference between fiction and truth.

III   The maiden was brought up in a castle by an illiterate nursemaid. Having learned to read and write, the maiden used her nursemaid to carry love notes to the Ineffective Knight.

IV   The king was almost executed for being in the wrong place at the wrong time. The Ineffective Knight's heroic, loyal speech saved him.

V   The maiden loved the Ineffective Knight with her whole heart. The Ineffective Knight initially seemed oblivious to her charms.

ADJECTIVE/RELATIVE CLAUSE EXERCISE:

**Circle the correct form of the relative pronouns in parentheses.
Remember: "who" replaces subjects; "whom" replaces objects.**

I   It was the prince (who/whom) we were discussing.

II   The king executed the duke, (who/whom) was a traitor.

III   The king suspected treason of (whoever/whomever) disagreed with him.

IV   The maiden, (who/whom) had bright blue eyes, fell for the knight hook, line and sinker.

V   The knight, (who/whom) she adored, gave her a kiss.

VI   The knight, (who/whom) finally noticed her, gave her a kiss.

VII   The maiden to (who/whom) the knight gave a kiss was transported with joy.

NOUN CLAUSE EXERCISES

**Identify all the clauses in the following sentences by class
(noun, adjectival, adverbial)**

I When the Ineffective Knight awoke, he looked at the sun to see what time it was.

II Whether he got up or not depended on what the day had in store.

III What he was going to do with the shoe that his horse had thrown had yet to be decided.

IV If he took the horse to the blacksmith that worked in the village, heaven knew how long the shoeing would take.

V What the Ineffective Knight really needed to do was get up, but he decided that the world would take care of itself if he left it alone.

**Simplify and clarify these sentences by taking the noun clauses
and expletives out of them.**

I What the outcome of the battle was could not be determined from the scout's report.

II Whether the casualties could yet be counted was dependent upon the condition of operations.

III From the return of the hippogriff batallion, it seemed probable that the battle was over.

IV Whether the hippogriff charge had won the day or merely lost hippogriffs was important to the cavalry's expectations of further fighting.

V It is certainly true that hippogriff charges terrify the enemy, but it is doubtful that they can survive retaliation by a squad of excellent archers.

VI It seems clear that a charge that greatly reduces the hippogriff cavalry is disastrous, but that they won the battle for us is gratifying.

ADVERB/SUBORDINATE CLAUSE EXERCISES:

Correct the following sentences.

I Unlike my mother told me, babies don't come from storks.

My mother told me babies come from storks, but they don't.
(Many other possibilities)

II I wish I had a golden carriage like Cinderella did.

I wish I had a golden carriage like Cinderella's.

I wish I had a golden carriage, the way Cinderella did.

III If the knight had married the maiden, like he said he would, she wouldn't be a single parent.

If the knight had married the maiden when he said he would, …

If the knight had married the maiden, the way he said he would, …

IV That maiden combs her hair like the queen pulled a dagger on her.

That maiden combs her hair as if the queen pulled a dagger on her.

V Unlike the war with the hippogriffs, the Ineffective Knight soundly defeated the invading army.

(This is an example of a sentence so scrambled it can't really be fixed—we don't know what happened. You can try, "Although he failed in the war with the hippogriffs, the Ineffective knight soundly defeated …" If that's what happened. Who knows? Let this be a warning to all of us.)

VI I can't see as the passage of time has made maidens any smarter.

I can't see that the passage of time has made maidens any smarter.

Combine the simple sentences below first into compound sentences, then into complex sentences with subordinate/adverb clauses. You may switch the order of the clauses any way you want, and you may use pronouns instead of repeating names.

(With each example, discuss the difference in emphasis in the varying versions of the sentence.)

I The Ineffective Knight was an odd fellow. His use of hippogriffs as airborne cavalry saved the kingdom from certain defeat.

Compound: The Ineffective knight was an odd fellow, but his use... **or** The Ineffective Knight was an odd fellow; all the same, his use...

Complex: Although/even though the Ineffective Knight... **(What happens if you don't** subordinate the oddities of the Ineffective **Knight to his use?)** The Ineffective Knight was an odd fellow, even though his use of... **(haven't you implicitly denigrated his achievement?)**

II The great recorder of the Ineffective Knight's deeds spent several years in jail for lying under oath. He wrote his epic poem to reflect on the difference between fiction and truth.

Compound: The great recorder of the Ineffective Knight's deeds spent several years in jail for lying under oath; meanwhile, he wrote... **or try** The great recorder of the Ineffective Knight's deeds spent several years in jail for lying under oath, but he wrote... **(Big difference!)**

Complex: While the great recorder of the Ineffective Knight's deeds spent several years in jail for lying under oath, he wrote... **or** Although the great recorder of the Ineffective Knight's deeds spent several years in jail for lying under oath, he wrote... **(Again, big difference!)**

III The maiden was brought up in a castle by an illiterate nursemaid. Having learned to read and write, the maiden used her nursemaid to carry love notes to the Ineffective Knight.

Compound: The maiden was brought up in a castle by an illiterate nursemaid, so, having learned to read and write, she used her nursemaid...

Complex: Because the maiden was brought up in a castle by an illiterate nursemaid, when she learned to read and write, she used... **(Note that this is a much stronger sentence** because it gets rid of the weak participial phrase "having learned to read and write.")

IV The king was almost executed for being in the wrong place at the wrong time. The Ineffective Knight's heroic, loyal speech saved him.

Compound: The king was almost executed for being in the wrong place at the wrong time, but... or The king was almost executed for being in the wrong place at the wrong time; however, the Ineffective Knight... (**Lots more emphasis on the ineffective knight.**)

Complex: Although the king was almost executed for being in the wrong place at the wrong time, the Ineffective Knight's heroic... (**Get them to try putting the "Although" in front of the Ineffective Knight's speech—the implication changes greatly:** Although the Ineffective Knight's heroic, loyal speech saved him, the king was almost executed...

V The maiden loved the Ineffective Knight with her whole heart. The Ineffective Knight initially seemed oblivious to her charms.

Compound: The maiden loved the Ineffective Knight with her whole heart, but... or The maiden loved the Ineffective Knight with her whole heart; however...

Complex: Although the maiden loved the Ineffective Knight with her whole heart, the Ineffective Knight... (**Emphasizes him**); or The maiden loved the Ineffective Knight with her whole heart, even though the Ineffective Knight initially seemed... (**Emphasizes her**).

ADJECTIVE/RELATIVE CLAUSE EXERCISE:

**Circle the correct form of the relative pronouns in parentheses.
Remember: "who" replaces subjects; "whom" replaces objects.**

I   It was the prince (who/**whom**) we were discussing.

II   The king executed the duke, (**who**/whom) was a traitor.

III   The king suspected treason of (**whoever**/whomever) disagreed with him.

IV   The maiden, (**who**/whom) had bright blue eyes, fell for the knight hook, line and sinker.

V   The knight, (who/**whom**) she adored, gave her a kiss.

VI   The knight, (**who**/whom) finally noticed her, gave her a kiss.

VII   The maiden to (who/**whom**) the knight gave a kiss was transported with joy.

NOUN CLAUSE EXERCISES

**Identify all the clauses in the following sentences by class
(noun, adjectival, adverbial)**

Noun clause   adjective clause   adverbial clause

I   When the Ineffective Knight awoke, he looked at the sun to see what time it was.

II Whether he got up or not depended on what the day had in store.

III What he was going to do with the shoe that his horse had thrown had yet to be decided.

(The adjective clause is part of the larger noun clause; it modifies "shoe." Discuss the effect of having one clause inside another.)

IV If he took the horse to the blacksmith that worked in the village, heaven knew how long the shoeing would take.

(The adjective clause is part of the adverbial clause.)

V   What the Ineffective Knight really needed to do was get up, but he decided that the world would take care of itself if he left it alone.

(The adjective clause is part of the noun clause.)

Simplify and clarify these sentences by taking the noun clauses and expletives out of them.

I   What the outcome of the battle was could not be determined from the scout's report.

The scout's report was so garbled that we (the general, the observers) couldn't figure out who had won the battle.

(Note that the noun clause took "us" out of these sentences.)

II   Whether the casualties could yet be counted was dependent upon the condition of operations.

We couldn't count casualties until we were sure the battle was over.

III   From the return of the hippogriff batallion, it seemed probable that the battle was over.

The hippogriff battalion returned, so we assumed the battle was over.

IV   Whether the hippogriff charge had won the day or merely lost hippogriffs was important to the cavalry's expectations of further fighting.

Hippogriff casualties determined the cavalry's plans for further fighting. (Making "The Cavalry" the subject immediately gets you into another noun clause: *The cavalry needed to know* whether the hippogriff charge was worth its casualties. In this case, the noun clause would be all right.)

V   It is certainly true that hippogriff charges terrify the enemy, but it is doubtful that they can survive retaliation by a squad of excellent archers.

Hippogriff charges may terrify the enemy, but they can't survive retaliation by a squad of excellent archers.

VI   It seems clear that a charge that greatly reduces the hippogriff cavalry is disastrous, but that they won the battle for us is gratifying.

The casualties of the hippogriff charge were disastrous, but we [whoever that is] are glad we won the battle.

IV. THE COMPOUND-COMPLEX SENTENCE

● **EXPLANATION**

HOW IT WORKS

A **compound-complex sentence contains two (or more) independent clauses and at least one dependent clause**.

EXAMPLE I

Adverb clause	Because hippogriffs fly,
Independent clause	wizards use them as allies
Independent clause	and witches use them as carrier pigeons.

EXAMPLE II

Independent clause	I once saw a hippogriff
Adjective clause	that had no wings;
Independent clause	its breeder was very disappointed.

EXAMPLE III

Independent clause	I have always thought
Noun clause	that breeding hippogriffs was exceptionally difficult;
Independent clause	griffins require crossing eagles and lions,
Adjective clause	which is difficult enough,
Independent clause	but breeding horses to the resulting cross inevitably yields varied results.

All the rules that apply to compound and complex sentences also apply to compound-complex sentences. So do the cautions. While a complex sentence never needs a semicolon, a compound-complex sentence very well may need one; substituting a comma creates the Comma Splice.

> The knight thrashed helplessly among the man-eating blackberry canes in which he had become hopelessly ensnared, the dark, cold eyes of the prowling hippogriff flashed dangerously.

The trick is to look for sentence subjects; if there are two, you'll need a semicolon or a coordinating conjunction.

> The knight thrashed helplessly among the man-eating blackberry canes in which he had become hopelessly ensnared; the dark, cold eyes of the prowling hippogriff flashed dangerously.

Be particularly careful when you use compound verbs in a complex sentence. Carelessness may lead to ambiguity. For example:

> The hippogriff flew over the castle where the beautiful maiden languished in miserable captivity and dove through her window.

Which is the compound verb: "flew and dove" or "languished and dove"? It makes a difference. Unless the maiden dove, make the sentence compound-complex:

> The hippogriff flew over the castle where the beautiful maiden languished in miserable captivity; then suddenly it circled, screamed viciously, and dove through her window.

WHY IT MATTERS

The compound-complex sentence is deceptively easy to write—you just keep piling information in until you run out of gas. Without real control, however, a writer may lose track of clauses or punctuation, and the result will be unclear. Until your students' writing becomes well-practiced and secure, they would be wise to limit the length of their sentences to twenty words.

SENTENCE STRUCTURE EXERCISES

PART I: SENTENCE COMBINING AND DE-COMBINING

Here are some sentences by Jane Austen (I & II) and Willa Cather (III & IV). Circle the verbs and underline the subjects in each clause. Then reduce each clause to a simple sentence. Consider the differences between your amended version and the original.

I   Captain Weston was a general favorite, and when the chances of his military life had introduced him to Miss Churchill, of a great Yorkshire family, and Miss Churchill fell in love with him, nobody was surprised, except her brother and sister, who had never seen him, and who were full of pride and importance which the connection would offend.

II   He turned away to recover himself, and when he spoke again, though his voice still faltered, his manner showed the wish of self-command, and the resolution of avoiding any further allusion.

III   The bare stone floor of the town and its deep worn paths were washed white and clean, and those depressions in the surface which the Acomas call their cisterns, were full of fresh rain water.

IV   One summer evening in the year 1848, three Cardinals and a missionary Bishop from America were dining together in the gardens of a villa in the Sabine hills, overlooking Rome.

Combine the following simple sentences below into
a) a complex sentence, b) a compound sentence, and c) a simple sentence.

I   James had a ball. The ball was red. James gave the ball to a woman. The woman had red hair. The woman was pretty.

II   Nancy rode a trike. She was sucking a lollipop. She ran into a tree. She swallowed the lollipop. She swallowed the stick.

III   My neighbor has a dog. The dog runs through my garden. The dog wrecks my flowers. I'm hiding behind a bush. I have a hand grenade. I'm waiting for the dog.

PART II: PHRASES VS. CLAUSES

A clause has its own subject and verb. A phrase does not. Sometimes phrases and clauses are interchangeable in meaning, but sometimes they are not.

**Change all the phrases that appear into clauses, and all the clauses into phrases.
Discuss the differences that may appear.**

I The man with two heads is my brother.

II The racehorse that has five legs is a puzzle to track fans.

III The cow that is jumping over the moon should have stayed off the sauce.

IV The man that had been given to hippogriffs for breakfast was in bad shape by noon.

V Tom hit the man who had four hammers.

**Convert the following complex sentences into long simple sentences
that have no clauses.**

I Arcadia, which is really a part of Greece, became a fictitious pastoral world in sixteenth century poetry.

II Nymphs, satyrs, and shepherds, who are the inhabitants of Arcadia, live in a state of pastoral *otium* that poets compare favorably with the *negotium* of the real world.

III The satyrs, who are creatures with goat's legs and men's bodies, spend most of their time chasing nymphs, who are virginal but seductive.

IV The nymphs, who have little else to do, spend most of their time running away from satyrs.

V The shepherds, who are supposed to be watching their flocks, actually fall in love with pretty shepherdesses and write them sonnets, which are fourteen-line poems in iambic pentameter that have rhyming couplets at the end.

PART III: STYLISTIC EXERCISES—DEVELOPING MASTERY

I Write a simple sentence that is 50 words long. Do not make it into a list of adjectives, nouns, or adverbs; use phrases (not *that* clauses!) as modifiers.

II Write a good simple sentence that is 20 words long.

III Write a 300-word essay/story all in simple sentences. Make as many of those sentences resemble sentence II, above, as possible.

IV Write a 300-word essay/story all in complex sentences that contain ONLY an independent clause and an adverb clause. NO relative clauses. NO noun clauses. Don't write in the first person, and do not name your hero.

Example

When the boy ran into the street, his mother was disturbed. He cried all the way home because he had seen a hippogriff across the street.

V Paste the story in IV onto a new page. Then insert a **bold-faced** relative clause in every sentence of the story. Punctuate carefully—this is a punctuation killer if you follow directions.

Example

When the boy ran into the street, his mother, **who was always anxious about his imagination,** *was disturbed. He cried all the way home because he had seen a hippogriff* **that had just done a crash landing** *across the street.*

PART I: SENTENCE COMBINING AND DE-COMBINING

Here are some sentences by Jane Austen (I & II) and Willa Cather (III & IV). Circle the verbs and underline the subjects in each clause. Then reduce each clause to a simple sentence. Consider the differences between your amended version and the original.

I   Captain Weston was a general favorite, and when the chances of his military life had introduced him to Miss Churchill, of a great Yorkshire family, and Miss Churchill fell in love with him, nobody was surprised, except her brother and sister, who had never seen him, and who were full of pride and importance which the connection would offend.

Captain Weston was a general favorite. The chances of his military life had introduced him to Miss Churchill, of a great Yorkshire family. Miss Churchill fell in love with him. Nobody was surprised, except her brother and sister. They had never seen him. They were full of pride and importance. The connection would offend that pride and importance.

II   He turned away to recover himself, and when he spoke again, though his voice still faltered, his manner showed the wish of self-command, and the resolution of avoiding any further allusion.

He turned away to recover himself. He spoke again. His voice still faltered. His manner showed the wish of self-command, and the resolution of avoiding any further allusion.

III   The bare stone floor of the town and its deep worn paths were washed white and clean, and those depressions in the surface which the Acomas call their cisterns, were full of fresh rain water.

The bare stone floor of the town and its deep worn paths were washed white and clean. The depressions in the surface were full of fresh rain water. The Acomas call those depressions their cisterns.

(Note that a restrictive relative clause has been removed and rephrased.)

IV   One summer evening in the year 1848, three Cardinals and a missionary Bishop from America were dining together in the gardens of a villa in the Sabine hills, overlooking Rome.

(This is a simple sentence. Discuss its excellent structure.)

Combine the following simple sentences below into
a) a complex sentence, b) a compound sentence, and c) a simple sentence.

I James had a ball. The ball was red. James gave the ball to a woman. The woman had red hair. The woman was pretty.

James gave his red ball to a pretty woman who had red hair.

James had a red ball; he gave it to a pretty red-haired woman.

James gave his red ball to a pretty red-haired woman.

There will be variations.

II Nancy rode a trike. She was sucking a lollipop. She ran into a tree. She swallowed the lollipop. She swallowed the stick.

Sucking a lollipop while riding her trike, Nancy swallowed it, stick and all, when she ran into a tree.

Nancy was sucking a lollipop while riding her trike; she ran into a tree and swallowed the lollipop, stick and all.

Sucking a lollipop while riding her trike, Nancy hit a tree and swallowed both the lollipop and the stick.

Many variations possible here.

III My neighbor has a dog. The dog runs through my garden. The dog wrecks my flowers. I'm hiding behind a bush. I have a hand grenade. I'm waiting for the dog.

I'm hiding behind a bush with a hand grenade, waiting for my neighbor's dog, which runs through my garden, wrecking my flowers.

My neighbor's dog runs through my garden and wrecks my flowers; I'm hiding behind a bush with a hand grenade, waiting for it.

I'm hiding behind a bush with a hand grenade, waiting for my neighbor's dog to run through my garden, wrecking my flowers.

Many possibilities here; note difference in subjects.

PART II: PHRASES VS. CLAUSES

A clause has its own subject and verb. A phrase does not. Sometimes phrases and clauses are interchangeable in meaning, but sometimes they are not.

**Change all the phrases that appear into clauses, and all the clauses into phrases.
Discuss the differences that may appear.**

I The man with two heads is my brother.

The man who has two heads is my brother.

The change from complex to simple sentence makes no difference to the meaning.

II The racehorse that has five legs is a puzzle to track fans.

The racehorse with five legs is a puzzle to track fans.

The five-legged racehorse is a puzzle to track fans.

Changing the clause to a phrase or an adjective makes no real difference to the meaning.

III The cow that is jumping over the moon should have stayed off the sauce.

The cow jumping over the moon should have stayed off the sauce.

The simple sentence is awkward. Participial clauses are often awkward; clauses are generally better.

IV The man that had been given to hippogriffs for breakfast was in bad shape by noon.

The man given to hippogriffs for breakfast was in bad shape by noon.

The simple sentence is okay, but original is stronger.

V Tom hit the man who had four hammers.

Tom hit the man with four hammers.

REALLY ambiguous! Who had those hammers? Who knows? Look out for prepositional phrases at the end of sentences.

Convert the following complex sentences into long simple sentences that have no clauses.

I   Arcadia, ~~which is~~ really a part of Greece, became a fictitious pastoral world in sixteenth century poetry.

II   Nymphs, satyrs, and shepherds, ~~who are~~ the inhabitants of Arcadia, live in a state of pastoral *otium* ~~that poets compare~~ compared favorably by poets with the *negotium* of the real world.

III   The satyrs, ~~who are~~ creatures with goat's legs and men's bodies, spend most of their time chasing virginal but seductive nymphs. ~~who are virginal but seductive.~~

IV   The nymphs, ~~who have~~ having little else to do, spend most of their time running away from satyrs.

V   The shepherds, ~~who are supposed to be~~ supposedly watching their flocks, actually fall in love with pretty shepherdesses and write them sonnets, ~~which are~~ fourteen-line poems in iambic pentameter ~~that have~~ with rhyming couplets at the end.

PART III: STYLISTIC EXERCISES—DEVELOPING MASTERY

No answers possible here.

I   Write a simple sentence that is 50 words long. Do not make it into a list of adjectives, nouns, or adverbs; use phrases (not *that* clauses!) as modifiers.

II Write a good simple sentence that is 20 words long.

III Write a 300-word essay/story all in simple sentences. Make as many of those sentences resemble sentence II, above, as possible.

IV Write a 300-word essay/story all in complex sentences that contain ONLY an independent clause and an adverb clause. NO relative clauses. NO noun clauses. Don't write in the first person, and do not name your hero.

Example

When the boy ran into the street, his mother was disturbed. He cried all the way home because he had seen a hippogriff across the street.

V   Paste the story in IV onto a new page. Then insert a **bold-faced** relative clause in every sentence of the story. Punctuate carefully—this is a punctuation killer if you follow directions.

Example

When the boy ran into the street, his mother, **who was always anxious about his imagination,** *was disturbed. He cried all the way home because he had seen a hippogriff* **that had just done a crash landing** *across the street.*